Handling Unwelcomed House Guests
A Straight Forward Guide to Relative Subversion

CHANCE BUCKMAN

To Shelley

Hope this might give you some top tips for any unwanted guests. Richard says please dont use it on us!

Love
Richard & Julie xo

Legal Disclaimer

Every effort has been made to accurately represent this product and its potential to rid your home of unwanted house guests. Though these suggestions are widely believed to assist in the evacuation of said unwanted guests, there is no guarantee your specific guests will be susceptible to the suggestions held therein. The success of said techniques depend entirely on the person, situation, deeply held beliefs, geographic and regional customs and unaccounted for extraneous factors.

Any claims of actual guest evacuations or examples of actual results are based solely on antidotal evidence. Your level of success in attaining the results claimed in this material depend on the time and effort you devote to the program, ideas, techniques mentioned, your knowledge of subversive practices and ability to improvise when our details go sideways on you. Since these factors differ significantly according to individuals, we cannot guarantee your success or empty spare bedroom/couch. Nor are we responsible for any of your actions, incurred legal fees, bail money, property damage, hospital bills, therapy sessions, funeral or other expenses not mentioned above.

In short, this book is intended solely for your amusement. If you truly have an unwanted house guest, please notify the appropriate authorities and institute whatever legal actions your local jurisdiction requires. Do not take the ranting of this author as any sound legal or family reconciliation advice or appropriate way to handle disagreements or uncomfortable situations. The information found within this book is humorous at best and pathological at worst.

Printed by CreateSpace.com

Copyright © 2012 by Chance Buckman

All rights reserved.

PAPERBACK   ISBN: 1479257168

PAPERBACK   ISBN-13: 978-1479257164

No part of this publication may be reproduced or transmitted in any form or by any means, electronic or mechanical, including photocopies, recording, and/ or by any information storage and retrieval system.

DEDICATION

This is dedicated to any one who does or has ever known the misfortune of a guest who over stayed their welcome.

CONTENTS

	ACKNOWLEDGMENTS	i
	INTRODUCTION	1
1	WHO DOES NOT QUALIFY AS UNWANTED GUESTS?	7
2	WHO DOES QUALIFY AS UNWANTED GUESTS?	13
3	AVOIDING THIS IN THE FUTURE	17
4	THEY'RE NOT LEAVING. NOW WHAT?	23
5	CREATIVE PLANS TO SEND THEM AWAY	29
6	PASSIVE AGGRESSION	31
7	INTERIOR DESIGNS	39
8	OUT ON THE LAWN	49
9	FAMILY SOLUTIONS	57
10	PSYCHOLOGICAL WARFARE	65
11	ROAD TRIP	77
12	EXTREME MEASURES	87
13	CHILDS PLAY	93
14	DEF CON 1	101
15	CONGRATULATIONS	103

ACKNOWLEDGMENTS

I graciously thank my wife and kids
for not kicking me out of the house.

My father & mother
for not kicking me out as a child.

and Jeff
for not kicking me out of his car
on the way to school so many decades ago.

I would also like to thank Scott Luper,
Vanessa Moreno, Preston, Hudson, Randy & Karen

HANDLE UNWANTED HOUSE GUESTS

INTRODUCTION

If you're reading this, I guess congratulations and condolences are in order. First, congratulations. You bought this book. Hopefully it'll provide you minutes and maybe even hours of reading pleasure.

If you have no house guests and are buying this in preparation for impending house guests, smart move. Read it – Learn it – Live it.

Actually living this book may not be your best bet. Use it if you need it. Keep it for reference, but otherwise, don't seek out opportunities to kick people out of your house.

CHANCE BUCKMAN

If you resort to inviting people over, solely for the sake of kicking them out, you'll be seen as passive aggressive. The neighbors won't like you. And that's exactly how my grandfather got kicked out of the Kiwanis Club back in '68.

If you're purchasing this book out of an extreme need for preparedness, good luck. I wish you the best. In the event of either a zombie or robot apocalypse I call dibs on your bomb shelter, because you're the exact person who makes it through those fictional disasters.

If however you're the poor sap who's buying this book because you've already got an unwanted house guest, my condolences. House guests can be a wonderful addition to a home – until they're not. They can instill in everyone a sense of nostalgia and a heart warming sense of kindness – until they no longer do. When those good feelings and benefits end, it's time to kick them to the curb.

Take comfort in the fact you aren't the first,

HANDLE UNWANTED HOUSE GUESTS

only, or even the most famous person to deal with this issue. Two examples quickly come to mind.

Newspaper magnate William Randolph Hearst had a sprawling mansion in California called San Simeon. His mansion was the place to be and be seen during the first half of the 20th century, especially if you were the rich and famous of Hollywood.

Rumor has it Hearst never asked anyone to leave San Simeon, but he made it abundantly clear when a guest had out stayed their welcome. He would begin moving the guest further away from Hearst' end of the table and closer to his impressively large fireplace. The longer you stayed, the closer you got to the lit, roaring fireplace, until it became impossible to eat, due to heat and lack of comfort.

In another example, famed British author Charles Dickens made the mistake of inviting equally famous Danish children author Hans

Christian Anderson to stay with his family in his home for two weeks in the 1850's. After five weeks of hints, suggestions and inconvenience, Anderson finally left the Dickens home and ruined a ten year friendship.

It's probably good for Anderson and the young Hollywood stars this book didn't exist. You're house guest however isn't that lucky.

In this book you'll learn the best, worst, and oddest ways to rid your house of your unwanted guest, but before we get into the actual techniques for extricating this blight from your home we'll discuss what does not qualify as an unwanted house guest. This will show you who not to kick out. Always resort to this guide if in doubt.

You'll learn the equally important, who does qualify as an unwanted house guest. Identification is the most important step.

Next we'll look at ways you can avoid this situation in the future. It may be too late this

HANDLE UNWANTED HOUSE GUESTS

time, but this chapter will help insure it never happens again. You may be getting victimized right now, but that doesn't mean you have to be a victim.

After that, we look at the normal routes you've undoubtedly taken before purchasing this book. If you find one in here you haven't tried, sneak away, try it now. If it works, it was worth the cost of the book, no one ever has to know. But I think we both do know, if it was that easy it wouldn't require a book written by a guy with a masters degree in clinical psychology.

From there we'll move onto the various, creative ways one can make the oblivious house guest accept the hint that they're no longer welcome. The options will move in order from the shockingly simple to the grotesque and highly ridiculous.

After that we'll wrap it up with a hardy congratulations for evicting the squatter and moving on with your life. Should an early option work and your unwanted house guest find their way onto some other kind, polite, completely ill prepared persons couch, feel free to skip promptly to the back patting at the end.

Once finished, feel free to go back and read the bizarre options you might have endured should the unwanted house guest have been completely oblivious to your subtle hints.

Oh, and once that's finished, please help out their next victim by lending or buying them a copy of this book. It's the least you can do, since you already know what they're in for.

Who knows, maybe when this book works for them, they'll eventually forgive you for not warning them about the house guest in the first place. Don't count on this to happen quickly though. The depth of hurt and pain they feel takes time to heal.

Remember how you feel about the people who didn't warn you about your house guest.

HANDLE UNWANTED HOUSE GUESTS

CHAPTER 1
WHO DOES NOT QUALIFY AS UNWANTED GUESTS?

It's important we get this out of the way before we move on. While it may seem like common knowledge for some, to the rest of us this list may hold grey areas.

SPOUSES – While your husband or wife may be unwanted by you at times, in the eyes of the law they're not "guests".

Kicking them out can end badly, resulting in divorce and division of property, for the lucky.

CHANCE BUCKMAN

For the rest, there's a good chance they'll find themselves in lock up over night with the only person capable of bailing them out unwilling to do so.

Or even worse, you might find out how he became calf roping champ of Ohio in jr. high or how she can still use the skills she learned on the way to becoming the All Around Ukrainian Arm Wrestling title holder four years in a row.

SIGNIFICANT OTHERS – In the same way you can't just kick out spouses, you can't go around kicking out significant others. Not if you're still with them anyway.

If you feel strongly, break up with them. Then kick them out. Chances are good the relationship wasn't going to last if you want to kick them out regularly.

And you can feel good knowing you saddled your former best friend with your pain in the tail ex because lets face it, if you kick them out, that's the first place they're heading.

HANDLE UNWANTED HOUSE GUESTS

In the long run all that really matters is you're done with the ex. And that friend owed you money they never intended to pay you. Take the win and move along.

CHILDREN UNDER 18 – You can kick them out but someone from some kind of three letter acronym social services department will quickly come around asking questions.

You know what you did to get the child. You knew in the vast majority of cases there was a good chance it was happening that night. You chose the night of fun, just deal with the 18 years of payment. And keep it in mind next time someone says they know a good way to spend the evening.

Hold onto your children, be happy, pay for their stuff and remember – they eventually pick the nursing home you go into. That alone is reason enough to pay for college, let them hang out until 25, and forget about kicking them out of your house as a teen.

CHANCE BUCKMAN
A PARTY FULL OF PEOPLE YOUR SPOUSE/ SIGNIFICANT OTHER INVITED – It could be a scrap booking party or the fantasy football draft. It could be a church group or a child's birthday party. Whatever the group, you might think it'd be hilarious to throw everyone out in the street during a party someone else has thrown. Resist the urge.

Not only will the spouse make your life a living hell, the people in the community will talk. But what does that mean to you?

When you actually have a legitimate unwanted house guest no one will help you, because everyone in your neighborhood will feel you deserve it.

Are they right? Are they wrong? Doesn't matter. Keep these people in your arsenal. You may need them at a later date, should you end up with an unwanted house guest.

You never know when the young divorcee across the street will be willing to take in your

HANDLE UNWANTED HOUSE GUESTS

leech to give the kids a new parent. It's not worth the risk to mess that up.

FRIENDS YOU INVITED OVER, WHO CHEER FOR THE OTHER TEAM – Be careful about this one. When the game's on, say in the fourth quarter, and people get to cheering, it's not the time to go kicking people out. That's how flat tires and IRS audits happen.

ANYONE NOT STAYING OVERNIGHT – They may be a pain, but they are your in laws and your spouse did invite them over. Give them the evening. They'll go home, and you'll know you have another option to drop the unwanted house guest off on, if the time ever comes.

At this point you know what does not qualify as an unwanted house guest. Let's see what does.

CHANCE BUCKMAN

HANDLE UNWANTED HOUSE GUESTS

CHAPTER 2
WHO DOES QUALIFY AS UNWANTED GUESTS?

You've seen who you can't kick out of your house with a clear conscience. If you find the people below in your house, kick away. Move them out and send them on their way. Enjoy a lack of guilt, knowing you did the right thing.

EX-SPOUSES – It goes without saying, ex spouses tend to get under peoples skin. If they didn't they wouldn't be ex's would they?

Here's the important thing to remember. When you're in a bad spot with an unwanted house guest, the ex won't help you out. In fact, they probably invited the deadbeat to stay at your house, when you think about it.

There are times to be nice and there are times you end up in the same room with your ex. Those two times are never the same.

SQUATTERS – What is a squatter? It's a person who comes into your house and stays – sometimes forever.

Usually squatters know all the weird laws they have at their disposal that allow them to continue squatting. Keep that in mind when kicking them out. They may know some law from 1862 that forces you to be hospitable.

What are the squatting laws? You'll need a squatters book for that. If you get one, don't let a squatter read it. They don't need any more ideas.

In general don't chance it. Consider the offer of anyone asking to come over in the same way you'd consider a vampire. Never invite them

HANDLE UNWANTED HOUSE GUESTS

into your house. They'll sleep all day, party all night, and completely drain you. You'd never invite a vampire in your home. Don't invite a squatter.

IN LAWS YOU DIDN'T INVITE – Especially if your spouse didn't invite them. Kick them out. Don't even think about it. Send them on their way. But didn't you say in the last chapter not to kick out in laws. I said not to kick out in-laws your spouse invited. Once their little baby says kick them out all bets are off. Go with what you feel.

In laws have a habit of staying beyond their welcome anyway. If you see floral print luggage in their hands, don't open the door. If you can help it, Don't even answer.

ANYONE STAYING BEYOND THE NEGOTIATED TIME – It's important to set up clear expectations with a house guest to help insure they don't become unwanted. We'll discuss this more in a future chapter, but in general set expectations up front. If the house guest violates them, don't hesitate to put them in the unwanted zone. This is a place they don't want to be. This is the place the ideas in the second half of this book go to grow up and wreak havoc.

Hearst had a unwanted zone near the fireplace. Dickens unfortunately did not. That's why it took five weeks to get Hans Christian Anderson kicked out on his considerable nose. Be Hearst, not Dickens.

CHAPTER 3
AVOIDING THIS IN THE FUTURE

Now you know what is an unwanted guest and what isn't. You may already have the misfortune to be in this situation.

If this doesn't describe you, let's look at what you can do in the future to insure you never end up with an unwanted house guest.

If you have an unwanted house guest, read along as well. It may help you figure out how you ended up with that unwanted guest and could potentially help you avoid the same mistakes in the future.

In either case, you can help insure you don't get guests in the future. And if you do, you'll know they won't end up unwanted.

NEVER ALLOW ANYONE IN YOUR HOUSE – I know. It's simple. It's elegant. It's does the job with grace and ease. If you never allow them in, they can't become guests. It's so amazingly perfect in design in fact, I don't even have to explain it further.

NEVER ALLOW ANYONE TO SPEND THE NIGHT – This one is akin to the last, however it opens up a little more chance you might end up with an unwanted house guest. If you must let them in, find a way to get them out quickly. Set a curfew when they first walk in the door. "I'm sorry. I have that thing really early. You need to be leaving soon." It's not elegant, but it gets the job done.

THAT'S AGAINST MY POLICY – This is a great catch all to get you out of trouble in all areas of your life. You just paid for the book

HANDLE UNWANTED HOUSE GUESTS

with the line above and saved a yourself fortune in reupholstery and food bills.

When someone asks to spend the night, say, "I'm sorry. That's against my policy." It's just that simple.

People ignore excuses, they see through them, they shoot holes in them. They may even ignore them. Excuses are flimsy.

Policies on the other hand are ironclad. They hold weight. No one questions a policy. They won't even think to ask, "You have a policy? Is it homeowners or personal?"

It won't even dawn on them to ask until they've already positioned themselves in some other poor, excuse making persons refrigerator. And at that point, what do you care?

THEY HAVE TO SPEND THE NIGHT BUT YOU DON'T KNOW THEM – DON'T LET THEM IN – I know. It seems simple enough, but squatters can be tricky. You may not even know their staying in your home until they've been there three days. They're just that crafty, but don't you have this secret weapon. That and if you don't answer the door it doesn't become an issue.

If however you're expecting that order of zombie apocalypse survival kits and you accidentally open the door to them, don't let them in. For any reason.

They could say they need a drink of water, or they need to use the restroom, or maybe they'll pull out the big guns and say the orphanage down the street is on fire and Lassie asked them to call 911. Don't fall for it.

Lassie's been in retirement since 92. And you don't have anything down the street from you besides a Walgreen's and Willum's Fried Chicken. Don't fall for it. And don't let them in.

NO ONE NIGHT STANDS – One night standers sometimes know squatters laws. Which ones? Don't chance it. Never invite a

HANDLE UNWANTED HOUSE GUESTS

one night stander home with you. In fact, in general it's probably a good policy to avoid one night stands.

Someone will end up pregnant then there's no kicking the kid out till college.

CONFIRM DEPARTURE BEFORE THEY ARRIVE – I don't mean, when are you leaving? I mean, give me the ticket number, the flight number and the gate number, so I can confirm and have you there early. If it's an open ended ticket don't let them stay.

Set clear expectations and boundaries before they ever show up. This alone scares off most would be unwanted house guests.

HAVE THEM READ THIS BOOK BEFORE THEY STAY – Send them a copy before they ever arrive. Make them pass a test. It's true in war, you don't tip off your enemy to your battle plans, but sometimes fear of the known is a powerful tool.

CHANCE BUCKMAN

We've seen how to avoid getting an unwanted house guests. Now let's look at what to do if you already have one.

HANDLE UNWANTED HOUSE GUESTS

CHAPTER 4
THEY AREN'T LEAVING. NOW WHAT?

Alright, they're in your house. They don't seem to be leaving. It looks like they're settling in. What do you do?

I should start by saying, it's always a good practice when dealing with unwanted house guests to have your locks changed, their bags packed at all times, and a new security alarm installed. One which they don't have the code.

This will make it easy to move forward should they decide on a whim to sit on the porch or walk out the front door for any reason.

It can be that simple. When they walk out the door, shut it, lock it, arm the alarm, walk away.

Because most of us aren't this lucky, let's start with the basics. If it wasn't established ahead of time, be straight forward. Ask when they're leaving. If they say never, skip to chapter 5.

You can always try to discuss the situation with them but lets face it, you know that's not an option or you wouldn't be reading this.

Hand your house guest this book and ask them to pick out the method most likely to get them out of your house. This alone could provide the desired effect.

Drop hints. These never work, but you can feel better later that you tried everything before moving on to the second half of the book.

Force them to confirm their departure and make them stick to it. This is a little more aggressive than most people want to be, but we all know, that's what gets everyone here in

HANDLE UNWANTED HOUSE GUESTS

the first place. In fact, I bet not answering the door when the house crasher first arrived is sounding pretty good right about now.

We've all seen the comedies where the house guest continually pushes out their exit. It's not funny in theaters, it's not funny in your restroom.

If they're reasonable enough, rent them a hotel room for a week or even a month and send them away. If they were reasonable though they wouldn't be clogging your kitchen sink with cottage cheese at 4 in the morning.

Another option to consider, you could arrange for another relative or friend to house them. I couldn't even type that without laughing. No one else wants them. They won't even answer your phone calls, now that they got the house guest off their couch.

This brings me to a good point, don't mention to any relatives that the unwanted house guest is staying with you or how long they've been there. It may feel good to commiserate over your troubles but you're tipping your hand to everyone around you, just how bad it would be to let the house guest in their home.

Never do that. Make people think you're friends. If a relative comes over, act like your unwanted house guest just came to visit. Act like you love spending time with them.

Make people think every time they see you with the house guest it's the best day you've had, since the last time you saw them.

Doing this will make it so much easier to offload your house guest to an unsuspecting relative who thinks they're in for an episode of Leave it to Beaver when they're actually in for a stay at Camp Crystal Lake from the classic horror flick, Friday the Thirteenth.

Side note, once you send the house guest on their way to someone else, don't answer when they call. It's doesn't help anyone.

HANDLE UNWANTED HOUSE GUESTS

So there you have it, the easy ways to send an unwanted house guest on their way. But you don't have an easy house guest. You know this stuff won't work. You already tried. So let's move on to the fun stuff – beginning with chapter 5.

CHANCE BUCKMAN

HANDLE UNWANTED HOUSE GUESTS

CHAPTER 5
CREATIVE PLANS
TO SEND THEM AWAY

It was mentioned in a previous chapter, but it's worthy information that bares repeating. When dealing with unwanted house guests, have your locks changed, their bags packed at all times, and have a new security alarm installed. One for which, they don't have the code.

You make your life easier should they accidentally wander outside for any reason.

It should also be noted that none of these options have been tested in a scientific double blind study nor are any considered sound legal defenses should the unwanted house guest come to any harm, which won't happen.

Therefore at the end of each of these "solutions" there will be a disclaimer, which I guess makes this a disclaimer about forthcoming disclaimers.

I wish you the best. I'm sure one of the options in this next chapter will work for you. If not, fret not. We have over fifty options for you to consider. These range from, "Why didn't I think of that?" to, "That's so simple. It could never work". From there the options move to, "I can't do that to someone I love (not the unwanted house guest)." to, "I can't believe you even suggested that. What's wrong with you, as a person?" I understand and believe me, I get that all the time.

We end with a section that you might think, "I can't do that to anyone, even the house guest." before ending on somewhat of a logical note.

I hope you enjoy your first set of options entitled "Simple Solutions or How to be Passive Aggressive".

HANDLE UNWANTED HOUSE GUESTS

CHAPTER 6
PASSIVE AGGRESSION

In this section we'll learn an important tool in ridding your house of not only unwanted house guests but, also solicitors, spouses, children, loved ones, and casual acquaintances.

Yes, in this section we see options that show how to be truly, pathologically passive aggressive.

You already know what passive aggressive is. If your mother or father didn't do it to you growing up, an old aunt or uncle did.

You know, that one goofy older person in the family who says horrible things to everyone while wearing an innocent smile. If someone gets upset by the relatives insult, they play it off as a joke. You know the people, we all do.

It may be weird and pathological. But a little pathology can sometimes be exactly what a crazy situation needs.

You shouldn't need to read any further than this section to get rid of your unwanted house guest. So let's move on to passive aggression in the home.

1

It's always nice to leave this book in common areas where your unwanted house guest congregates. When possible, put it where they sleep. When they get out of the shower, have it waiting on the counter. Where ever they turn, show them how you feel without saying a word.

It can warm your heart knowing they get the point without having the confrontation.

(Disclaimer: Do not leave books where they can be tripped over or can in any way cause an obstacle. This could lead to injuries.)

HANDLE UNWANTED HOUSE GUESTS
2

It's also nice to be polite to the rest of the family, especially when it drives home the point that the house guest is an inconvenience to everyone around them.

Try this one, leave notes around the house for them to find; notes you've written to loved ones apologizing for allowing the house guest to stay. When possible detail your disgust for the house guest.

Don't give the guest an opportunity to think you're being fake. Leave no doubt in their mind. Make your genuine disgust come though on the paper.

You can feel good knowing people love to read someone else's mail and your family will appreciate you've left little notes for them.

(Disclaimer: Notes and paper products of any kind can leave nasty paper cuts. Do not leave notes lying around where people can cut themselves.)

CHANCE BUCKMAN
3

You've bought the book. Now let them see you reading it. Sometimes this can be enough.

Your unwanted house guest will ask what you're reading because on top of everything else, they like to butt into your business.

When this happens, you can take one of two approaches. Your first option is to say, "You should read this, it's a great book. It tells how to throw out house guests like you. You know, the kind of people no one can get rid of".

This will convey a straight forward message and it's not like you wanted to tell them. They drug it out of you.

When this happens you can feel good knowing their question was heard and if you're lucky, they will hear the anger and contempt in your response.

(Disclaimer: Do not read while walking, thinking, practicing gymnastics, some forms of martial arts or performing tasks on heavy machinery. This could cause a variety of injuries.)

HANDLE UNWANTED HOUSE GUESTS
4

You always have a second option when asked what you're reading. Throw it (the book) at them.

Please note: It's important to have multiple objects at the ready should you decide to employ this method. It's really doesn't matter what.

(In some cultures the preferred throwing items are slippers or chanklas. In others a throwing star or wok.)

When throwing items at the unwanted house guest, scream "O pah" when possible. Make it sound like innocent fun while aiming for sensitive soft tissue.

People love that (the O pah, not soft tissue injuries).

You can feel good knowing their reflexes have been thoroughly tested, probably for the first time since jr. high. And they know now your level of accuracy with common household items.

Practice before hand to make a good impression. No one wants a person with bad aim throwing things at them. Someone's bound to get hurt.

(Disclaimer: Do not throw household items at people with the intention of causing soft tissue injuries. This is no laughing matter. Soft tissue injuries hurt and they take time to heal.)

5

This option is the height of passive aggression. As your house guest goes through their normal day in your home, charge them LOUDLY for everything they do.

By this, I mean for example, follow them to the restroom door. As they go in to use the restroom shout. Light. 2 dollars. Fan. 4 dollars. Sink. 4 dollars. Toilet flush. 4 dollars.

You can easily see how much fun this can become, especially if you include the whole family and charge the house crasher for every single activity they partake. Your kids will love to join in.

Everyone loudly scream out charges for everything they do. Let the kids set their own prices.

Everyone gets tired of creditors. Be the creditor who doesn't sleep, the law has limits to what a

HANDLE UNWANTED HOUSE GUESTS

creditor can do and when they can call. Those laws don't extend to your house guests.

You can feel good knowing they are gaining a firm grasp of home economics, a subject they no doubt failed in jr. high. You can also learn what it feels like to be a national bank, charging fees. It feels pretty good, doesn't it?

(Disclaimer: There are laws against price gouging so try not to engage in that activity. There are also laws governing collection agencies. I'm pretty sure federal laws do extend into your house. Keep that in mind if you get serious about this option.)

6

This one is always fun. Start giving away their stuff to Good Will or some other worthy charity. While you do, complain that charities have standards and you don't think they'll take the house guest's crap.

Shame is always a good, sound technique. This also serves the purpose of lightening the load when you have the opportunity to get them out of the house.

CHANCE BUCKMAN

You can feel good knowing you're helping your house guest free themselves of the consumer chains that bind them and their action figure doll collection won't be all over your living room floor anymore.

(Disclaimer: Goodwill and other charities do good work. Oh, and giving away other peoples things is legally "frowned upon" in most jurisdictions.)

HANDLE UNWANTED HOUSE GUESTS

CHAPTER 7
INTERIOR DESIGNS

I'm sorry the last section didn't offer any solutions. This next section surely will. From basic passive aggression we now move into plans generally based in the home, although the first option gets the guest decidedly out of the home. It's still not hardline enough to be moved further down the list.

7

If the first several options didn't work, maybe you can find them a job, preferably at a competing firm. This is only an option for those who feel guilty about kicking a house guest into the streets. I myself have never found this to be a problem.

CHANCE BUCKMAN

Once they receive their first paycheck, charge rent – exorbitant rent.

Remember, if they're in your house over six months you can count them as a dependent on your taxes.

You can feel good knowing they're getting back on their feet and you're recouping some of your losses. Be sure you include the toilet seat and the refrigerator door they broke in your balance sheet.

(Disclaimer: I'm not an accountant and generally have no idea what I'm talking about when it comes to matters of money.)

8

This next option is considered in most countries too cruel to attempt. Everyone pays when you employ this tactic, but lets face it. Sometimes when teaching lessons, everyone has to learn.

Lock your TV on either the Matlock channel or the Murder She Wrote channel.

There are other great options as well, like Quincy M.E., Barnaby Jones and Diagnosis Murder.

HANDLE UNWANTED HOUSE GUESTS

Be careful though, in the same way kidnapping victims can get Stockholm Syndrome and begin to sympathize with their captors, a person subjected to nothing but Angela Lansbury can find themselves addicted.

You can feel good knowing they gained some culture and an understanding of how TV stars of the past solved mysteries and who knows, maybe they'll decide to move to a fictional town to fight crime in a geriatric manner just like their newfound heroes.

(Disclaimer: The detox process to bring a person down off Angela Lansbury can be painful, even deadly. Seek professional help.)

9

With this next option, things get serious. Have Sports Center cut off, then Fox Sports, then cable, then the rest of your utilities.

Cold water showers can work wonders on a person. It can even inspire in them a deep desire to leave.

Keep in mind, you can turn off power to their end of the house using your breaker box, this will leave them in the dark while everyone else remains relatively without inconvenience.

This method can also be used to drive them through a house and out the front door, like cattle through a branding chute.

You can feel good knowing how much they'll appreciate their next victims house. Chances are their next victim won't think to cut off utilities, until they get your copy of this book.

(Disclaimer: There are fees associated with having utilities disconnected/ connected. Also, have your breaker box inspected by a licensed electrical contractor before attempting to cut off individual breakers. Safety first.)

10

You'll pull out more stops with every step further down this list.

You've cut off the utilities and they haven't left. Why not remove all paper products in their end of

HANDLE UNWANTED HOUSE GUESTS

the house and replace them with stacks of poison oak leaves?

Understand though, you'll have to hide all print media and paper goods in the house. There are few things a crafty as person without paper products in the restroom. As a precaution, remove towels from their restroom as well.

You can feel good knowing your house guest is getting in touch with nature and learning a valuable lesson about plant identification.

(Disclaimer: Some individuals are extremely allergic to poison leaves. Always have an Allergist perform a full allergy test before replacing paper products with poison oak leaves.)

11

STOP FEEDING THEM. Feed the rest of the family but don't set a place for the unwanted house guest.

Why is this not option number one? Because unwanted guests find food, somewhere, somehow they always do. If you cut off food after other options fail you'll be more vigilant.

If not setting a place for them doesn't work, which it won't, start eating during their late afternoon nap or their favorite show.

Stop buying food for the house and eat out. Eventually they'll have to go out for food and when they do, you can be there with packed bags, changed locks and set alarms.

You can feel good knowing you've honed their survival skills and you and your spouse can get a much deserved break from cooking.

(Disclaimer: Don't starve people. They get cranky and whiney. Also they could develop health problems. And a cranky whiney person with health problems is tough to listen to.)

12

When the last option doesn't work, move onto this one. Take the lose. Show them they won. You've broken down and you're feeding them again.

Are you serious? Just like that? Yes. Because, unlike the last option, you decide what they eat. Here's where it gets fun and humiliating.

HANDLE UNWANTED HOUSE GUESTS

Feed them sandwiches that would disgust a Fear Factor contestant. Pick the weirdest parts of the strangest, market sold, animals you can find.

A mexican market should be able to help with this request. Go to the local "michoacana" and ask for the special. I promise, it will be "special". It's still food. It provides the same nutritional value as the food the rest of the family's eating.

They'll have "texture issues" with the food options. So please video as this itself should provide a lasting record of the time you spent together.

You can feel good knowing your house guest is receiving three nutritious meals a day while gaining a greater appreciation of other cultures delicacies. You can also rest easy knowing you're feeding them for pennies on the dollar compared to what you were paying when they were getting into the Frito's and ice cream.

(Disclaimer: Look over the allergist test to make sure they aren't allergic to any of the animals you're feeding them. Ox is usually a safe bet, especially if they eat hamburgers.)

CHANCE BUCKMAN
13

There's a glitch in human programming that allows people to freely and openly discuss the things they fear most. Just ask. They'll tell what scares them. Once they do, play on their fears.

At least you can have fun with the extermination.

They're afraid of Santa Claus? Volunteer to host the convention for Santa's local 438 at your house. Be sure to video the response.

They said they're scared of timber wolves? Who isn't? Release four in their bedroom at 2 AM. Be sure your camera has night vision.

Whatever their fears, prey on them and make them feel relieved to be out of your hell house of horrors.

You can feel good knowing you helped conquer their fears and you'll have fun in the process.

(Disclaimer: Phobias are scary. Lay out plastic sheets before helping people confront phobias. It makes for a slippery escape and there's a good chance they'll lose their bowels on your floor.)

HANDLE UNWANTED HOUSE GUESTS
14

This is only for those who enjoy mans best friend.

Open an attack dog school in your living room. Tell your house guest everyone has to do their part. Hand them a padded suit. This alone should send them fleeing.

You don't have to actually open a school but they do need to see an advertisement and a coupon. And you will have to rent nine German Shepards for the afternoon and practice a German accent.

You can feel good knowing they appreciate your commitment to safety and the proper training of K9 units everywhere and who knows, one of the dogs may give them a nip on the way out.

(Disclaimer: Don't train any attack dogs unless you've received the proper training and licensure. This is not a get rich quick option worth exploring.)

15

This one will take some online investigation if you, like me, don't have a background in engineering.

CHANCE BUCKMAN

If your unwanted house guest sleeps on your couch, attempt this beautiful practical joke commonly employed by undergrad engineering students. Check youtube for examples.

Go to your local auto salvage yard. Procure four vehicle airbags and place them under the couch. Then set off your new experimental couch while your unwanted house guest is soundly asleep. For an added bonus, post the video online, please.

I can't tell you how it ends, but here's a hint. The airbags throw your guest off the couch and into the living room wall – hard.

You can feel good knowing they received the same sort of rude awakening they've subjected you to. Not to mention the hours of enjoyment your video will provide to millions of laughing viewers. You're providing a service when you really think about it.

(Disclaimer: Vehicle airbags are legitimately dangerous. Have you ever been slapped in the face with one? Also, walls are legitimately dangerous. Have you ever been slapped in the face with one?)

HANDLE UNWANTED HOUSE GUESTS

CHAPTER 8
OUT ON THE LAWN

I'm sorry the last two sections didn't work out. I could've sworn they would. There's no need to fret though, if the last chapter didn't work, this next chapter surely will.

In this section we move from in home tactics to maneuvering your unwanted house guest out onto the lawn, making them someone else's problem. And we all know there's nothing nicer than a former house guest, especially one that's someone elses problem.

As said before, be prepared for these opportunities. Remember your new mantra. Change the locks, pack their bags, change alarm codes.

CHANCE BUCKMAN
16

This is one of the more simple if not ridiculous options, but it also has a high rate of success.

Have the entire family run outside and point in the air. Then one of you yell, "What is that thing?".

People in cars will stop and stare, you'll feel like a complete idiot, but eventually temptation and curiosity will get the best of your house guest and you know what curiosity got the cat? That's right, it got them kicked out of your house for sticking around past their welcome.

They'll eventually run out to see what that thing is. When they do, creep to the house and slam the door behind you. Make sure no child's left behind.

Once they're outside they're the cities problem. If you can, try to have their bags packed and sitting by the front porch, where they can't be seen until the house guest tries to get back in.

You can feel good knowing they got their stuff back and maybe they even saw that thing.

HANDLE UNWANTED HOUSE GUESTS
(Disclaimer: Don't try "what is that thing?" at busy intersections. The city will hold you responsible for the wrecks. And I was serious about not leaving children behind.)

17

This one is so simple it's often overlooked. When the house guest gets up to use the restroom at 2AM, call the police about an intruder. As they hand cuff the guest and take them away, swear you've never seen them before, except on America's Most Wanted.

You can feel good knowing they could be getting the help they need for whatever problem they may have, over the course of the next 12 to 18 months and you don't have to deal with their midnight giggle fests over their restroom exploits.

(Disclaimer: Don't claim someone was on Americas Most Wanted if they weren't. People take that seriously. Also, be sure to use nightlights to mark common walkways in the dark. This can save people from unnecessary accidents. Also, sometimes people do laugh in the restroom.)

CHANCE BUCKMAN
18

This one seems a little involved, but it should get you the results you desire.

When the unwanted house guest goes to sleep, have their door plastered over, trapping them in their room. When they wake up for their 2 AM giggle filled restroom run they'll discover their predicament. With their mind still foggy, chances are they'll crawl out the window into the yard.

Soon as this happens, call the police about an intruder in the yard.

You can feel good knowing they'll have a sense of accomplishment when they realize they thought outside the box to get out of their doorless room and you'll feel good knowing their problem solving skills are improving.

(Disclaimer: Always allow enough time for plaster to set properly. Otherwise, you'll have a gooey mess on your hands that'll never really look right. Also, don't crawl out windows unless absolutely necessary. Especially if you're in a horror film.)

HANDLE UNWANTED HOUSE GUESTS
19

This option is especially good in neighborhoods that have community events. It means you don't have to advertise.

While your unwanted guest sleeps, take all their possessions and put them on the front lawn in a garage sale. Price everything to move fast.

When they run out to get their stuff, tell them it's their shift, then lock them out. It's just that simple.

You can feel good knowing you recouped some of your loses in the first three hours of the sale – before they woke up. And who knows, they may make enough money to get a Southwest Airlines Super Saver Fare.

(Disclaimer: Again, selling other peoples possessions is legally "frowned upon" in most jurisdictions. Also when operating a garage sale attain the proper license and inform buyers you do not provide a warranty on any items sold.)

CHANCE BUCKMAN
20

How about you get the family together to perform nightly fire drills, complete with sirens and lights.

It will mess with their ability to sleep and your kids will love it. At the end of the day, a weak sleep deprived person is an easy person to break.

As a side note, the nightly kid enhanced fire drill was considered by acknowledged experts the most grave form of torture at internment camps. To this day, turning the lights on and off while a child yells fire drill, still causes some grown men to break out in tears and loose control of their bodily functions.

Before the fire drill starts, be sure to leave the front door open. In their terror stricken stupor the house guest might just run out the front door, at which point you slam it shut, set the alarm, and call the police about a strange man in the front yard screaming fire.

(Disclaimer: There are laws against filing a false fire alarm. So contact the fire department ahead of time to let them know it's a drill.)

HANDLE UNWANTED HOUSE GUESTS
21

This is one of those feel good options. Ask them to help you do some extreme labor job, like helping a neighbor reroute their sprinklers or helping the local elementary school dig up all the plants in their flower beds.

Once they've started their assigned task, set out their bags and the payment for their job and leave.

You can feel good knowing they did an honest days work for 12 dollars and who knows, maybe the neighbor did need their sprinkler rerouted. Maybe the elementary school hated the flowerbeds the kids just planted on Earth Day. You never know until someone asks you to stop.

(Disclaimer: Do not perform improvement projects on public or private property without permission and get the appropriate local zoning permits before work begins. Also, there are federal laws governing minimum wage restrictions and IRS requirements concerning wage reporting.)

CHANCE BUCKMAN
22

It's always fun to help history buffs and lets face it, kids love the show.

With this in mind, why not invite the local civil war reenactment group over to practice their night warfare battle – in your living room, at 2 am, where the unwanted house guest sleeps.

You'd be amazed how stealthy that group of 50 year old dentists and computer programmers can be. Especially when it's for a good cause.

You can feel good knowing everyone learned a little something about civil war firearms and your unwanted house guest will never again make fun of the hard working men of the 7th infantry reenactment group.

(Disclaimer: Submit your house guest to a full medical physical before planning your next living room civil war reenactment. Also, inform local authorities of the event so no one worries.)

HANDLE UNWANTED HOUSE GUESTS

CHAPTER 9
FAMILY SOLUTIONS

I'm sorry the last three sections weren't fruitful. This next section may prove difficult, but surely it'll work.

From the front yard we'll now move to the yards and homes of the hardest people in your life to fool. Your family.

It'll be a tough sale. Everyone involved already has knowledge of the house guest. Some family members may never speak to you again, for even mentioning the idea. You'll be talked about at family parties for years. But in all honesty, isn't it worth it for the chance to offload your house guest?

CHANCE BUCKMAN
23

Maybe you can just send them to another relative. Put in the time. Talk up the different options. Once the unwanted house guest decides between the aunt in Boca Raton and the high school friend in Aspen for his new digs, buy the ticket. It's the least you can do, to get them out of your house.

You can feel good knowing they get to see the country from the window of that bus, on their way to a better life, with close recreation areas and to be honest, you never really talk to that aunt or that friend anyway.

(Disclaimer: When purchasing cross country bus tickets, always make sure the bus has a restroom.)

24

Here's an option that should warm your heart, and cool your guest bedroom. How about shame your unwanted house guest into taking care of a sick relative, especially if the unsuspecting victim's in the hospital. It's a win win win. You'll be giving your sick relative their own little helper. The

HANDLE UNWANTED HOUSE GUESTS
unwanted house guest might even get a renewed sense of responsibility. And you'll get their lazy honk off your couch.

Don't think about this too much or you'll start feeling bad about yourself again, and that's what got you here in the first place.

Instead think about the stain on the restroom ceiling they caused; the one requiring a haz mat scrub down.

Consider that your kids don't have to play the pull my finger game again until Christmas two years from now, when you're finally allowed back into the relatives house you forced the house guest on. Also keep in mind the time your house guest walked in on you and your spouse in bed because he thought you were watching a movie, instead of making one.

Those reasons should ease your mind about your decision to sell your friend or relative up the river in their time of need.

You can feel good knowing the house guest and the sick relative may have a series of fun, life changing events that bring them closer and teach a lesson. I'd guess the lesson could be, don't give relatives your house keys when you go in the hospital.

(Disclaimer: Entering a house for unapproved reasons, even with keys, could constitute some sort of law infraction in certain jurisdictions. Also, allowing the unwanted house guest to use the hospitalized persons restroom could constitute destruction of property.)

25

In a very similar vein to the last option, consider which relatives are out of town. Wait for your opportunity, offer to stop by and collect the mail, you know, check on things.

Once they've left town, make the great house guest migration into their den. By the time the out-of-towner gets back, the unwanted house guest should be settled and harder to get out of the house than bubble gum in a three year olds hair.

Will the out-of-towner be upset? Sure. Will they be stressed? Maybe. But remember, they just got back

HANDLE UNWANTED HOUSE GUESTS

from vacation. Who's better prepared to handle your former house guest than a person refreshed?

You can feel good knowing maybe they'll take the house guest on the kind of vacations you could never afford, while they were eating you out of house and home.

(Disclaimer: As with the last option, Entering a home could constitute some sort of law infraction, although now that I think of it, maybe you can send the unwanted house guest a book on squatters rights – once they're situated in someone else's house.)

26

Is your house guest staying with you because of some sort of relationship problem with a spouse or significant other?

If that's the case, congratulations, there's an easy solution. Force a reconciliation, even a fake one if you have to.

Lie to the loved one if necessary. Tell them they're all the house guest talks about.

One special caveat, don't let them know the house guests' discussion always gravitates to the significant others shortcomings, complaints, accusations, and insurance plots.

Say whatever it takes to force a reconciliation. Eventually everyone will be better off.

You can feel good knowing they took the chance and worked hard on their relationship. And you'll have time to reflect, in your empty living room, kitchen, guest bedroom and restroom.

(Disclaimer: Never, ever involve yourself in someone else's relationship problems, that's how innocent people end up hurt.)

27

If your house guest doesn't have current relationship problems, don't worry. They surely have former significant others.

Invite the unwanted house guest's ex's over. Does an ex have a current spouse? Are they in a serious relationship? That's not your problem. Maybe there are unresolved issues in need of clearing.

HANDLE UNWANTED HOUSE GUESTS

Who knows, maybe those crazy kids will rekindle their romance. Maybe the house guest could move out with the ex or the spouse will find them together and reconcile their own situation.

Either way you can feel good that you helped give love a second chance... or that the ex's spouse will finally get the anger management help they need.

(Disclaimer: Cheating is never ok. I neither advocate it, nor engage in it, so don't ask.)

28

Since we're on the subject, maybe all they need is love. Why not sign your unwanted house guest up on any of a number of great dating websites.

You know the house guest well, maybe too well. Surely well enough to fill out a profile. In fact, as self sabotaging as your house crasher is, you'll fill out a better profile than they would anyway.

Don't make them out to be the most interesting person in the world, or dare I say Ricardo Montalban. Give a fair but slightly positive online impression of them. Include an actual picture.

Inmates on death row are inundated with marriage proposals, surely your unwanted house guest can find someone.

Here's the key though, you don't have to find them a soulmate or the one. All you have to do is get them out of the house for a date. Once you drop them off, remember the basics, changed locks, packed bags, alarm codes.

Hopefully it'll be a wonderful evening. Maybe they will find love, but honestly, once they're out your door, they're off your couch and that's the true goal of this book.

You can feel good knowing they've jumped back into the dating pool and who knows maybe they're ready to find love again. You can also stretch out on your couch again and get your guest bedroom back, not to mention your restroom.

(Disclaimer: There are rules against filling out dating profiles for other people. Never violate the terms of service on websites, especially dating websites – Jesse.)

HANDLE UNWANTED HOUSE GUESTS

CHAPTER 10
PSYCHOLOGICAL WARFARE

I'm sorry the last four sections didn't fix your problem. In all honesty, the last section was a long shot. We all had to know that. This next section however will surely work and even if it doesn't, you're gonna have fun with these next offerings.

Before we start, you may be asking yourself, it's not ok to engage in psychological warfare, is it? Surely not. You aren't at war, you're vacating a vermin from the premises. In these cases any means, psychological or otherwise, are completely permissible.

CHANCE BUCKMAN
29

Our first option requires the use of a video camera, preferably one with a bright light.

We've mentioned this option in connection with other and we'll mention it again. Why not follow your unwanted house guest around and record their every move? Tell them you're filming a documentary on people who stay beyond their welcome. Tell them they're doing you a favor.

Every time they do anything have camera lenses ready to adjust in front of them – and film them literally everywhere.

Chances are good they'll leave, but even if they don't, you might make the money back posting their horrible life on the internet and getting advertisers.

In fact, video every one of these options as you try them and become an internet sensation. There's really no accounting for taste where internet video viewing is concerned, but one thing's pretty certain.

HANDLE UNWANTED HOUSE GUESTS

The internet loves nothing more than to see an idiot get a horrible surprise they never saw coming. Butter the kitchen floor, jump out of the freezer, you name it. If an idiot gets hurt, it will be viewed. If you film it. They will come.

You can feel good knowing you've introduced your unwanted house guest to the world and in the process documented against future litigation.

Who knows, maybe a crazy old benefactor or their next spouse will notice them online and decide they need your house guest as their own. It's sounds far fetched, but it's not impossible.

If approached to give away your unwanted house guest, don't check references or backgrounds, just send them away with the first offer you get.

(Disclaimer: Human abduction is a very serious problem and should not be taken lightly. What this book advocates is finding your unwanted house guest a new roomie they can hang with; a roomie you never caught the name of.)

CHANCE BUCKMAN
30

I'll admit, this one's cruel but so is the discussion they had with your toddler about the non existence of awesome holiday beings.

The day after the lottery numbers are announced, buy a ticket with the winning numbers and give it to the house guest. Tell them they've won.

Send them into hiding while you get the paperwork ready.

You can feel good imagining all the fun they'll have deciding how to spend their imaginary money while sitting in that utility less cabin you rented by the lake. Who knows, maybe they would've even bought themselves a house.

(Disclaimer: While this option does not advocate lottery subversion, it should be noted, trying to cheat the lottery is a very serious problem with stiff penalties. Never try to cheat the lottery. The house always wins.)

HANDLE UNWANTED HOUSE GUESTS
31

Is your unwanted house guest a fan of social media? Why not access their facebook page and make all sorts of wild claims and dangerous, reckless comments.

Who knows, maybe some of the people in their friends list are actual friends. If so, maybe they'll have your house guest committed for their own safety.

If the house guest denies the comments, even better. Swear you watched them write it all out and you begged them to stop.

Maybe the house guest will be so distraught, they'll have themselves committed. This is highly unlikely, but there is a good chance they'll become violent when confronted and that's another sure fire way to receive the mental health help you neither wanted nor requested.

You can feel good knowing they're finally receiving help, even if it is based on false information and let's face it, people don't come back to a place that had them committed.

(Disclaimer: Mental health issues are serious. If you or someone you know suffer from mental health issues you probably won't seek help, but take comfort knowing eventually your loved ones will seek it for you. Also, do not violate the terms of service of social media websites. These sites have teams of people paid to do nothing but figure out who you really are.)

32

How about give your unwanted house guest their very own unwanted roommate?

You could hire an actor, preferably one specializing in horror film screams and martial arts fighting. Just have them jump out of dark corners and scream or let them practice that highly dangerous muy thia stunt for their next low budget, masterpiece on your unsuspecting, incredibly out of shape house crasher.

HANDLE UNWANTED HOUSE GUESTS

Perhaps recruit a nice, yet intense multi war veteran in need of a new set of ears to hear every single violent story from his time in three different wars. He fought on the ground in 119 engagements and guess what, he'll recall in vivid, graphic detail every one of them for your unwanted house guest.

As a side note, don't let the vet tuck your kids into bed. He won't tell war stories but it's a safe bet the only songs he'll know are "Ghost Riders in the Sky" and those racist march cadences learned in Korea.

You can feel good knowing the actor is getting experience, the veteran is being heard and maybe the unwanted house guest is learning a thing or two about close quarters combat from both of them. Who knows, you may have just given them the information that could save their life one day.

(Disclaimer: It is important to take care of our war veterans, they made the supreme sacrifice for our country and for that they deserve our thanks. Also never engage in martial arts sparring without proper warmup and stretches. Such reckless behavior can result in muscle pulls and cramps.)

CHANCE BUCKMAN
33

This one seems pretty basic. Considering the level of inconvenience this unwanted house guest puts you through, the last thing you want to do is become their personal assistant or errand person.

With this in mind, do not under any circumstances refill their prescriptions. If the house guest wants or needs their prescriptions badly enough, they'll go get them. This will send them out of the house, making them no longer a guest. Set the alarm.

This won't actually happen. It's much more likely they'll happily go off their psych meds, which makes them unstable, and easier to mess with. Once they're completely off any psych medications, start this list again. They won't remember earlier attempts and they might fall for an easy one now.

You can feel good knowing the doctor will have an easier time, since they can start medications with a clean slate and your medicine cabinet will have less space since, lets face it, they were taking most of your medication anyway.

HANDLE UNWANTED HOUSE GUESTS

(Disclaimer: Never withhold medications from individuals who are actually in need. Also, do not under any circumstances take medication that was not prescribed to you. Chances are you'll wake up in the middle of the night with a horrible case of dry mouth – or worse.)

34

This option plays to your individual tastes. You've always wanted to start a hobby. Take some time for yourself and start it now. But do yourself a favor and make it an uncomfortable hobby for your unwanted guest. Especially since you'll include them. Everyone loves to feel included, right?

For instance, you've always wanted to start raising bees. Do it in their room. It's good to know what upsets bees, so you can make sure you never do. Read up on it and make the house guest try each one and report to you the results.

You thought about woodworking or welding? Setup your saws or torches next to their bed, or couch. Have them stand beside the saw or welder while you work. It's always good to have a little helper.

Do you like spiders, but never had the time to explore your fascination? Now's your chance. Set up your terrariums right over their head while they sleep. Show your house guest the different parts of the spider as you learn them. They may be skidish around your new friends but don't worry, they'll get over that after they wake up covered in spiders.

Ever thought about learning Mandarin Chinese? Spend your practice time sitting next to the unwanted house guest loudly learning. Ask the house guest how your pronunciation is. Make them learn with you.

Whatever you want to do, do it. Don't let the rules of public decency stop you. Your house guest sure didn't worry when they stayed beyond their welcome.

You can feel good knowing you taught them an appreciation for your new found hobbies and it's always good knowing when they move out, you'll

HANDLE UNWANTED HOUSE GUESTS
have a jump start on your hobby – once you have the extra space – and time.

(Disclaimer: Hobbies of any kind can be extremely dangerous. Never attempt hobbies. If not for your own health, for the patience and attitudes of your loved ones, who'll surely get sick of you talking about your new found love.)

35

This option could be interesting and fun for your whole family. Does your unwanted house guest believe in ghosts?

If so, why not set up hidden speakers in their room and let your youngest child sit up all night whispering death threats into the microphone you set up in their room.

If the child and the unwanted guest fall asleep, wake the guest, by screaming in their face as you run a chicken claw down their face. Be sure the room is pitch black, for effect.

CHANCE BUCKMAN

Oh and get out of the room before they can get up. Otherwise you'll have to play it off as a joke... and what's the fun in that?

Be sure to increase the severity of the encounters until the house guest decides they've had enough and move.

You can feel good knowing you gave them experiences they can recall to the friends and relatives who still speak to them, for years to come and let's be honest whatever you have to use to clean off the couch after their other worldly encounter is not the worst thing they've done to your upholstery.

(Disclaimer: Never use a chicken claw without properly cleaning it. No one wants to get avian flu, especially from a ghostly encounter.)

HANDLE UNWANTED HOUSE GUESTS

CHAPTER 11
ROAD TRIP

I'm sorry the last five sections didn't do the trick. If we're being truthful, it was fun, wasn't it? I'm afraid if your unwanted house guest didn't succumb to last chapters options, they're tough. They're veterans to the house guest game. They know the tricks, but all is not lost. Everyone, including your home crasher, has a common, exploitable weakness. Everyone loves a road trip.

In this next section we'll look at ways you can lure unwanted guests from the home with the promise of a road trip, errand or secret traveling ploy. If you play your cards right, they'll never see it coming.

CHANCE BUCKMAN
36

Every unwanted house guest loves Walmart, as much as they love reality shows about auto repossessions and hoarders. Take advantage of this weakness and invite them to Walmart Super Center with you.

Once inside, it's easy to give them the slip. I don't know if it's true but I heard a lady once got lost in an Alabama Walmart for 18 months, before she found her way out.

You can feel good knowing your unwanted house guest has literally everything they need, under one roof and what they don't have you no longer have to provide – a place to crash.

(Disclaimer: No one has ever been lost in Walmart for 18 months. Also, it is ill advised to live in Walmart. Eventually you would feel like all the employees and customers were unwanted house guests. Who would want that?)

HANDLE UNWANTED HOUSE GUESTS
37

Hopefully they've already become an internet sensation, with your help.

Strike while the irons hot and sign them up for a Big Brother/ Survivor/ Wipe Out/ Fear Factor / Biggest Loser style reality show. Everyone wants to be famous. And you know it'd be fun to watch them humiliate themselves, even for one afternoon.

By the way, after the interview, DON'T BRING THEM HOME. Leave them with their new found friends and producers.

You can feel good knowing you gave them a shot at their dream to be a reality star and you'll have so much fun watching them fail trying.

(Disclaimer: Reality shows can be dangerous. Never involve yourself in any activities requiring medical and legal releases. It always means they know something you don't.)

CHANCE BUCKMAN
38

This next option can be gross, but it's almost always fun. Feed your unwanted house guest extra strength chocolate flavored, chewy caramel style laxatives. Then take them on a road trip.

At some point thirty minutes out, it'll surely hit them. They need to stop somewhere. Try to time the restroom emergency within five miles of a state maintained, roadside rest stop. When they get out to answer the call of the colon, pull away. It's that simple.

You can feel good knowing they probably met some new trucker friends and they may be seeing America as Eisenhower intended. Who knows, they might even become the King (or Queen) of the Road.

(Disclaimer: No matter what all teen comedies say, it's never ok to give a person laxatives for the sake of a joke. A funny, funny joke. Also, keep in mind your tax dollars pay for the upkeep of state maintained rest stops. Utilize public funds wisely.)

HANDLE UNWANTED HOUSE GUESTS
39

This option is thankfully not gross, and not costly. How does your unwanted house guest feel about travel? Have they mentioned a city they loved? Treat them to a $59 Southwest Airlines plane ticket. Pick the city, buy the ticket online and give them the surprise; the beautiful, house clearing surprise.

Have their bags packed so there's no time to think about your generosity. In fact while you're packing for them, why not pack the half used economy sized bottles from your restroom. Everyone needs the essentials of hygiene, even if your house guest doesn't partake of such pleasantries in your house.

You can feel good knowing they're embarking on an adventure and that adventure will begin at the airport security check when the security officer realizes their carry on's full of bottles, decidedly over the 3 oz. limit.

(Disclaimer: Always follow FAA and Homeland Security laws and regulations regarding air travel, especially the rules concerning 3 oz. bottle size.)

CHANCE BUCKMAN
40

Some unwanted house guests won't fall for a random act of kindness. They'll think it's some kind of trick, and they'll be right. If you fear you have one of these suspicious sorts on your couch, consider changing it up a little and handling the same situation this way.

Buy a Super Saver Fare but pick a random city and an early bird flight. Wake them from a sound sleep and run them to the car with everyone packed. They won't suspect as much with kids involved.

From your house drive straight to the airport. Pull up to their departure gate and take their (already packed) luggage from the trunk.

While you do this, have the rest of your family jump out with signs and yell surprise. Give your newly liberated house guest kisses on the cheek and wish them luck. Remind them to empty their pockets as you push them through security. They'll be too stunned to protest until they're halfway to Provo, Utah. Make sure this is a one way ticket.

HANDLE UNWANTED HOUSE GUESTS

If they do protest, don't worry. They're out of your house. Whether they get on that plane or not, your problem's solved. And I hear the airline industry will be bouncing back any day now. Maybe they can accept one these future jobs. They are right there after all.

Be sure to take the spouse and kids out for congratulatory breakfast and take the opportunity to profusely apologize for letting the unwanted house guest stay in the first place.

You can feel good knowing Provo's supposed to be lovely this time of year and without the house guest, things will be looking brighter around your house as well.

(Disclaimer: Always obey loading and unloading zone regulations at airports. They get pretty serious about those sorts of things. They're trying to avoid people leaving unwanted house guests on their curb. It's bad for business.)

CHANCE BUCKMAN
41

If the airport plan doesn't work for you, this one will be more difficult, but it can be fun as well.

Take the unwanted guest on vacation with the family. Once they're out of the house, you're home free, leave the car with them inside if you have to.

If you want to take it a step further and ensure the unwanted house guest will be occupied for the foreseeable future, head down to Galveston Island on the coast in Texas. Why Galveston? There are Greek and Liberian shipping vessels always in need of first mates with your house guests specific qualifications, whatever those may be.

Pull up to the docks, hand them a fifty dollar bill and ask them to go purchase the tickets for the dolphin cruise while the family parks the vehicle.

From there you just hide and watch from a safe distance. Lock your doors. Before they get to the end of the dock, neighborly sailors will have taken care of the rest.

HANDLE UNWANTED HOUSE GUESTS

If Galveston is a multi day trip for you, don't worry. Every major waterway has an international port. Go to the most convenient drop off and enjoy the local, tourist approved flavor.

You can feel good knowing you gave them the opportunity to see the world in a way boat people and refugees only dream of. Also, your family will enjoy spending the day at Galveston on the Strand, not to mention the bodily function free, ride home.

(Disclaimer: port and dock areas can be dangerous, especially for families. Rusty nails may carry tetanus. Wet or splintering docks may cause slip and fall or impalement dangers. Be careful. There's danger everywhere. Tetanus is no joke.)

CHANCE BUCKMAN

HANDLE UNWANTED HOUSE GUESTS

CHAPTER 12
EXTREME MEASURES

I'm sorry the last six sections didn't rid you of your problem. Hopefully your family at least got to enjoy the time away from the house and the sunny locales mentioned in the section above.

If the last chapter didn't work chances are good you're dealing with either an extreme house guest with experience beyond their squatting years, or you found yourself in the company of the shut in house guest.

It should be noted, the term shut in isn't meant in any derogatory manner. It's in no way meant to describe the elderly or those with any mental or physical challenges. The definition shut in, in this case, is only intended for those with anxiety or agoraphobia issues. More specifically, those who fear leaving a house.

This brand of house guest is fairly rare. They had to have gotten to your home in some way. They most likely either came via mass transit or you had the misfortune of having some jackass relative leave them on your doorstep while you were in the hospital. Either way, you don't have a shut in on your hands.

This assumes of course, you haven't traumatized the house guest causing a form of anxiety disorder or post traumatic stress, which by number 43, what are the chances, right?

Also, shut in house guests are extremely susceptible to psychological warfare tactics, making it more likely you're dealing with a professional. If so, I'd like to offer my condolences.

Removing a house guest of this level is extremely

HANDLE UNWANTED HOUSE GUESTS
difficult, but not impossible. Extreme house guests call for extreme measures and it's no coincidence this chapter's called extreme measures. It came by it's name honestly.

If you do find yourself in the company of an extreme house guest, this next section's definitely for you.

42

Nothing else worked so far, why not make up a disease the entire family has? The crazier the better. Legionnaires isn't used much these days. You could even pick a disease people don't get – like Parvo.

If possible have them wake up to find your friends, dressed in haz mat suits, taping plastic sheets to the walls and demanding everyone stay put.

Your house guest is a rebel. Can't tell them what to do. Chances are good they'll sprint from the house in their (wrong) day of the week underwear, screaming like a Legionnaires, Parvo stricken banshee.

You can feel good knowing they take precautions to protect their health and the cleanup will be easier with the plastic sheets and haz mat suits in place.

(Disclaimer: Always take precautions when running outside, especially without a shirt or shoes. The threat of West Nile Virus is very real as is the possibility of foot blisters. Our feet are our friends.)

43

Why not appeal to their sense of altruism? Tell your house crasher they have to leave since you're selling your home – to join the Peace Corps. (For the record, the Peace Corps. won't allow you to volunteer others for service – I've checked.)

Make a show of packing and moving furniture out. Even hold a going away party. They'll think it's for you. Turns out your friends and family are celebrating your unwanted house guests departure.

You may feel bad knowing you lied, but you know you're never inviting them over again. They won't even know where you live from now on.

HANDLE UNWANTED HOUSE GUESTS
You can feel good knowing you gave them a party and an appropriate send off and moving the furniture out was necessary anyway as most of it has to be cleaned now.

(Disclaimer: Investigate the best bargain as carpet and furniture cleaning companies can have widely different price quotes for the same work.)

44

If the last option didn't work maybe it's time to consider actually joining the Peace Corps.

I hear they do great work and honestly, after everything you've been through with your unwanted house guest you'll be so happy to be done with them, you may not even turn down the crazy assignments .and you'll be helping others.

Another great point to consider, in your new position you're more likely to be a house guest, rather than have one.

You can feel good knowing you're making a

difference and your house guest can't stay in your house anymore, because you don't have one.

(Disclaimer: Before doing missionary work in foreign countries ensure you and your family are up to date on your vaccinations. All of them. Even ones you don't think you'll need. Also, never attempt to sell your house without the help of a licensed professional.)

45

Water boarding. I don't know what it is or how you do it, but I hear it's effective.

You can't really feel good about this one. No one wins.

(Disclaimer: Don't ever water board anybody)

HANDLE UNWANTED HOUSE GUESTS

CHAPTER 13
CHILDS PLAY

The last seven sections didn't work for you? Really? If this is the case, I'm truly sorry, one of these should've done the trick by now.

If you still have your unwanted house guest, it's time to consider some cruel and unusual punishment. I hate to even commit this to paper for fear it could slip into the wrong hands with catastrophic consequences.

In this next section we'll look at the most psychotic option ever offered. That's right, I'm talking about – children Dun Dun Dun (ominous theme music).

CHANCE BUCKMAN
46

Along the same lines as the last option, have your youngest play a game I like to call, "Why?"

You've played the game. You know how it works. Ask a simple question, then continue to follow up the answer with the word, why. Again, sit back and watch the mind numbing fun begin.

Is your unwanted house guest a skilled Why player? If so, teach your kiddo ways to avoid shutdowns. Teach redirections and other upper level tools to keep the game going.

It's powerful. It's cruel. You didn't ask them to still be in your house after all this time. They deserve what they get.

You can feel good knowing your unwanted house guest is learning the techniques needed to deliver a great interview or to accept a job in exploitative journalism. And your child can learn what it feels like to be heard for 11 hours straight.

HANDLE UNWANTED HOUSE GUESTS
(Disclaimer: Never give a child undivided attention for eleven straight hours. It will set them up for disappointment in later years. At most, give them forty five minutes at a time, followed by fifteen minutes of alone time. It's best for their development. *** I'm not a doctor and therefore am not qualified to make any statements period***)

47

Not a big fan of the game or questioning options? How about make your unwanted house guest feed your baby their jarred baby food?

When doing so, it's fun to always suggest the baby will eat better if the house guest tries first.

Use statements like, "Do you want the mean ole unwanted house guest to try your strained Brussels sprouts? Do you?"

After a few days of horrible strained meals, come to the house guest while they sleep. Place an open baby food jar near their head. Make sure it's a jar of the most sickening flavor you can find.

Eventually they'll be traumatized to the point solitary confinement won't seem like such a bad option. They'll definitely have to get away from babies for the next several years.

You can feel good knowing the house guest finally helped out around the house and possibly gained a greater appreciation for baby food manufacturing techniques.

(Disclaimer: Baby food is difficult to get out of carpet, upholstery, interior paint and hair. Keep this in mind when placing an open baby food jar near a sleeping persons head.)

48

This next option moves from one end of the child to the other. No one wants an unwanted house guest changing their child's diaper. I wouldn't suggest that, but the house guest can stand by while you change diapers.

They can be at the ready to hand you whatever items you might need. They can hold the diaper

HANDLE UNWANTED HOUSE GUESTS
while you pretend to inspect matters. Pretend to smell the diaper then ask their opinion. When possible cram the offending material (not in their face) but near enough to cause dry heaves.

Once the unwanted house guests' gag reflexes are tested, it becomes easy to utilize the steps from the last option. Once they fall asleep, leave the heave inducing diaper near their head.

Before doing so, take no chances. Remove all family heirlooms and keepsakes from the involved room.

Know that they'll potentially throw up. They'll probably fly into a rage and they may tear things up, but at some point the unwanted house guest will either run to the door for dramatic effect or at least stick their head out a window.

Whenever this happens, be ready. Push them out the door or through the window. Then remember your old stand by, changed locks, packed bags, new security codes. Lock it up and leave them in the yard. The police will take it from there.

You can feel good knowing they've finally come to terms with their suppressed rage and the police will take them somewhere capable of examining their issues at length and remember, whatever damage they cause will be no more than they caused during their stay.

(Disclaimer: Never put human feces in anyones face. The chances of contracting diseases are high. Also, do not take rage issues lightly. If you encounter someone with rage issues contact your primary school counselor at once. Also, primary school counselors are not helpful in areas of actual mental illness concern.)

49

Oh, the humanity. Why would you do this next option to anyone? Hasn't the unwanted house guest been through enough? Well that depends. How much have they put you through while occupying your couch, guest bedroom, kitchen and restroom?

HANDLE UNWANTED HOUSE GUESTS

For this option, build a box around your television so no one can gain access to the television control buttons or power cord. Then hide the TV remote control.

What could possibly come next? Play the Teletubbies on a continuous loop. That's right, 24 hours a day, 7 days a week. Constant Teletubbies, night and day. I'm nauseating myself just writing this.

My guess is your unwanted house guest problem will be solved within 6 hours. No matter how experienced the foe, the match will be yours.

You can feel good knowing the house guest is gone. There is no positive aspect for them in this case. In fact, I feel for what the house guest is about to be put through and believe me, I don't ever side with a house crasher.

(Disclaimer: Do not subject others to this form of media torture. There's only so much the human mind can be expected to withstand.)

CHANCE BUCKMAN

HANDLE UNWANTED HOUSE GUESTS

CHAPTER 14
DEF CON 1

I'm sorry the last eight sections didn't rid you of your unwanted house guest. I could've sworn the section on child focused torment would cause even the most ardent house crasher to flee. I intentionally saved this option, I call def con 1.

50

Nothing else has worked. The unwanted guest dealt with everything you've thrown their way. You've given them some of your best shots but you're still staring at their lowriding sweat

CHANCE BUCKMAN

pants, bouncing in front of your refrigerator. It's time to consider one last option.

Sit down and ask them what's happening in their life. There may be a good reason they need to be in your house, or there may be something you can help with.

You may be surprised at the response you get from having a straight forward, frank discussion with your unwanted house guest.

Sometimes this is the easiest thing to do. Why is it listed number fifty? Because it's more fun to exhaust all other possibilities first.

You can feel good knowing you treated them as an adult, a peer. Although you do have to admit, the more childish options were more fun to carry out.

(Disclaimer: Only start a frank discussion when you're prepared to have a frank discussion. Also, hydrate. Always hydrate. The last thing you want during a frank discussion is dry mouth.)

CHAPTER 15
CONGRATULATIONS

Congratulations are in order. If you're reading this you've hopefully ridden your home of your unwanted house guest.

You've performed an amazing feat most aren't capable of, freeing your home of the unwanted house guest, through means of subversion and passive aggression. It was fun wasn't it? I'm certain your children enjoyed the experience as well.

You've done a wonderful job. You should be proud. Throw a party, a "We Threw Them Out", party. Enjoy the extra space, the extra food, the extra restroom time now available. You've definitely earned the extras.

If this book didn't help you to that end, feel confident no book would've. It may be time to seek the help of a professional exterminator, one who specializes in the evacuation of unwanted house guests.

Hopefully you're not one of the very unlikely few who ended up with a house guest impervious to this amazing and comprehensive list of methods and techniques.

I thank you. You've made it to the end and are no worse off. Some might even say you're a little better. I greatly appreciate you and your decision to purchase this book. Your choice means the world to me.

*** In this final sentence, please let me reiterate. This book is solely for your enjoyment. It's not literally intended as any kind of true or legitimate advise.

Please use safe and responsible judgement in everything you do, especially when vacating your home of an unwanted house guest.

HANDLE UNWANTED HOUSE GUESTS

CHANCE BUCKMAN

Printed in Great Britain
by Amazon